WORKING TOGETHER

HOW TO BECOME MORE EFFECTIVE IN A MULTICULTURAL ORGANIZATION

George F. Simons

CRISP PUBLICATIONS, INC.
Los Altos, California

WORKING TOGETHER

HOW TO BECOME MORE EFFECTIVE IN A MULTICULTURAL ORGANIZATION

George F. Simons

CREDITS
Editors: **Michael Crisp and Francine Lundy-Ruvolo**
Designer: **Carol Harris**
Typesetting: **Interface Studio**
Cover Design: **Carol Harris**
Artwork: **SeSe Egan**

Copyright © 1989 by Crisp Publications, Inc.
Printed in the United States of America

Crisp books are distributed by:
   ODT, Incorporated
   P.O. Box 134
   Amherst, MA 01004
   (413) 549-1293

Library of Congress Catalog Card Number 88-92728
Simons, George
Working Together
ISBN 0-0961931-85-8

ABOUT THIS BOOK

WORKING TOGETHER can be used in several different ways, including:

- **Self Study.** This book is designed so that you can use it on your own. It will involve you actively as an individual learner from beginning to end. The basic concepts are highlighted by examples and exercises so that you will retain them and be able to apply them appropriately.

- **Group Learning.** You can learn more by doing the exercises in this book with a partner or a group of people. It will be especially helpful if your partner or members of your group come from different cultural backgrounds.

- **Training.** Add the capabilities and leadership of a skilled trainer and this book enables you to explore the person-to-person and intergroup issues provided by cultural differences within a work team or organization. As a self-study workbook it can also be used to train those in remote locations who cannot attend home office training sessions.

- **Education.** On the high school, college or university level, the book will supplement classroom work in the social sciences by enabling students to investigate their attitudes about cultural diversity and then develop useful interpersonal skills.

There are several other possibilities. One thing for sure, even after it has been read, this book will be looked at—and thought about—again and again.

PREFACE

Working with people who look, believe, or act differently from you, may be difficult or uncomfortable. You don't know what to say, or what to expect, or simply find yourself inhibited, self-conscious, or even fearful when those from other cultures are around you.

Certain people may not react when you speak to them, or perform in the way you expect. What moves you doesn't seem to motivate them in the same way.

Maybe you sincerely believe that you do your best to treat everyone equally and fairly, but others inform you that you are insensitive, unfair, or prejudiced. Perhaps some have even accused you of discriminating against them.

It might be that you are an "outsider" in someone else's culture. You may be angry or frustrated about not being taken seriously or not being able to "read between the lines" to find out what you need to know to do your job well.

Perhaps you see the rich variety of people in your city and in your workplace and are saddened by the misunderstandings that keep your city, your country or your business from being what it could be. Imagine what these people, with all their experiences, skills, and ways of looking at things, could create if they were allowed to reach their potential!

This book provides you with an opportunity to do something about understanding other cultures. The future will bring more diversity, not less. Public and private leaders all over the world face the challenge of uniting different individuals and groups to reach common goals. The best leaders learn to draw unique contributions from each group. The future of your world depends on it.

You can become a leader, whether you are a manager in a multinational corporation, a government employee, or simply work or live side-by-side with another human being different from yourself.

WORKING TOGETHER will help you to understand and respect people of other cultures and be understood and respected by them. Its three main sections will show you how to interact with different kinds of people. Follow each step and you will learn to:

1) **Manage your mind**—master how you think about yourself and others,

2) **Manage your words**—learn to speak and listen to people with different backgrounds, and,

3) **Manage your unspoken language**—know how to pay attention to the non-verbal language of ''where, when and how'' you do things.

So, pick up your pencil—this is both a ''read'' and a ''do'' book—turn the page, and let's get started!

George F. Simons,
Senior Consultant
ODT, Inc.

WHAT DO I WANT FROM THIS BOOK?

If you know what you're looking for, you're much more likely to find it. Below is a list of goals which this book could help you achieve. Check those that are important for you. Then you will be able to focus on specific goals as you read this book and have a sense of satisfaction and accomplishment when you have finished reading this book.

I HOPE TO:

☐ Work efficiently with people of other backgrounds.

☐ Avoid offending those different from me.

☐ Feel more secure around people whose values, opinions and priorities are different from mine.

☐ Learn to appreciate, understand and gain cooperation from those who talk and act differently.

☐ Build an organization that encourages the full potential from the different groups within it.

☐ Learn to influence those who are in the dominant culture to treat others fairly.

☐ Combat prejudice and injustice in whatever form it takes.

☐ Know how to put my values about cultural diversity into practice.

☐ Be more comfortable traveling to other cultures.

ADD YOUR OWN:

☐

☐

☐

iv

CONTENTS

SECTION ONE
MANAGE YOUR MIND

Managing how you think about yourself and others who are different from you requires a fresh way of looking at things. This section will help you step outside of yourself and your normal way of thinking.

Section One will:
- Ask you to take a look at how culture makes you different from others.

- Teach you how your mind automatically judges others and what you need to do to keep prejudice from hurting you and them.

- Encourage you to explore situations in which your discomfort with others may make it difficult to deal with them.

- Teach you how to manage your feelings of fear and suspicion in order to work together effectively.

WHICH SIDE IS UP?

Below is a map of the world. Although it is turned "upside down," it shows accurately the *true size* of the world's continents and nations in relation to one another. This map, called the Peters Projection*, gives us a more honest picture of the world than older versions. Can you pinpoint on this map, where you, your parents, and your ancestors came from? What about where the "roots" of some of your neighbors and co-workers are from?

Does this new image of the world change how you see the importance of certain continents and countries? How does it feel to look at the world from a different point of view? Where does that put you? What thoughts come to mind?

It occurs to me that: _____

_____

_____

_____

_____

_____

WHICH SIDE IS UP? THERE ARE MANY WAYS TO LOOK AT IT!

---

*For more information on the Peter's Projection, see Resource Section.

WHO'S IN THE CENTER OF OUR UNIVERSE?

Three hundred years ago people were debating whether the earth or the sun was the center of the universe. Although scientists eventually proved that the earth revolved around the sun, many people still did not accept it. Even today, for most of us, the sun still "rises" in the east and "sets" in the west. We naturally tend to put ourselves in the middle of the universe.

Each of us also looks out from the center of a personal and cultural universe. From this *egocentric* or *ethnocentric* point of view, we (and the group we belong to), are in the middle. Other people and events revolve around us. It's easy for us to assume that the way we see things is the *real* way things are for everybody, or the *real* way things *should* be.

The truth is that people have many personal and cultural points of view. Even within your own culture, you are the only person with exactly your outlook! The world is *polycentric*—that is, there are as many midpoints as there are people to look out from them.

It is easy to say, "walk a mile in someone else's shoes," but it is not easy to do. You can observe, study, talk, listen, imagine, and empathize with others but *your* eyes, ears, mind and personal experiences still interpret what you take in. The next page will illustrate this point.

4

AN EXERCISE IN PERSPECTIVE

Think of some people whose differences are hard for you to accept or understand. Pick one of those people and think for a moment about the things that make that person different. Think especially about things that irritate you. Then shift your point of view. Imagine that you could be in this person's body and mind. You now have his or her eyes, mind, and feelings. You now see your true self from the "center" of another's universe. What would irritate you about you if you were that person? Jot down three things that you think another person would find hard to understand or accept about you:

1. _____

2. _____

3. _____

Good try! You won't know how accurate you were however, unless you were able to ask the person that you had in mind. However, you did something just as important. You stepped out of the center of your universe into someone else's, and opened your mind to the possibility of seeing things from another point of view. If you practice this at least once with each new person you meet tomorrow, you will be on your way to understanding diversity.

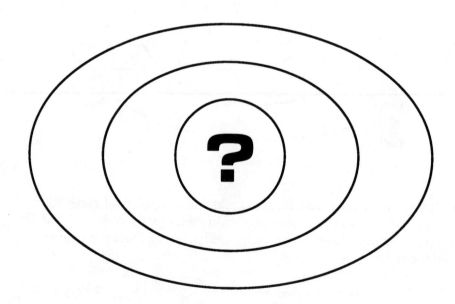

WHO'S IN THE CENTER? IT DEPENDS ON WHO'S LOOKING!

WHAT MAKES PEOPLE DIFFERENT?

Following are two factors:

1. BIOLOGY

No two people (excluding identical twins) have the same genes. We look different and have different kinds of bodies to work with. Biology determines our sex and the color of our skin, hair, and eyes. Sometimes it limits us physically as, for example, when a person is born without sight, or is disfigured, or without the use of a limb.

Most biological differences don't mean much in themselves. It's what people make of them that really counts. This means we need to pay more attention to the second factor, culture.

2. CULTURE

Culture is how we are raised to view and practice life. It is the inevitable result of rubbing elbows with one segment of the human race. It shows up in how we make, do and celebrate things. You can see it in how we talk to ourselves about ''us'' and ''them.'' It tells us who ''we'' are and gives us attitudes about ''them,'' the people who are different from us. It tells us what should be important as well as how to act in various situations.

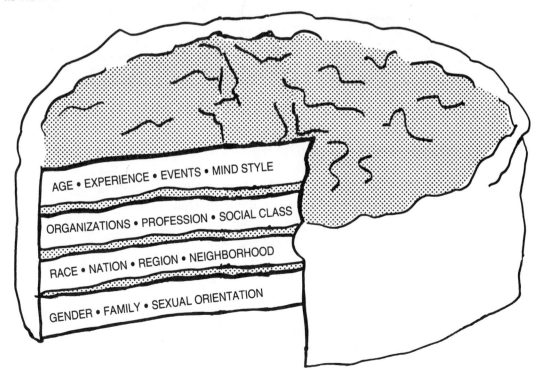

AGE • EXPERIENCE • EVENTS • MIND STYLE

ORGANIZATIONS • PROFESSION • SOCIAL CLASS

RACE • NATION • REGION • NEIGHBORHOOD

GENDER • FAMILY • SEXUAL ORIENTATION

ONE CULTURE OR MANY?

A few people belong to only one or two cultures. Most of us are like a slice of layer cake. We have several cultural layers. Each teaches us something about how to interpret everyday events and how to behave. Our ''layers'' make us like other people in some ways and different from them in others.

Imagine you are a slice of cake. Using the picture below, write on each layer some of the things which make you culturally different from other people at work or in your neighborhood. Start with the basics, like gender, race, where you or your ancestors came from, religion, etc. Look at the cake on the previous page if you need help thinking of things.

MY LAYERS

WHEN IT COMES TO PEOPLE, *DIFFERENT IS NORMAL*

A normal human being is a person with a variety of biological and cultural distinctions as well as an individual personal history that sets her or him apart from every other person. Each of us is a unique recipe.

The candle on the drawing of the cake should remind us that each of us has some light to bring to the world. Every person has something to contribute.

WHAT WE MAKE OF DIFFERENCES

Cultural differences become important because we make them so. People pay more attention to certain differences than others. Following are differences that were not in the exercise on pages 7 and 8. In your opinion, how do people in your community or workplace tend to see these differences? Rate each category below as:

1 = little or no importance; 2 = somewhat important; or 3 = very important

RATING

☐ **Occupation**
How we view ourselves as a result of the kind of work we do. (Engineer, Tradesperson, Machinist, Retailer, Artist, Marketer, Supervisor.)

☐ **Sexual Preference**
Unconscious or conscious choices we make about whom we desire for sexual partners or the choice not to have sexual partners. (Gays, Lesbians, Heterosexuals, Bi-Sexuals, Celibates.)

☐ **Social class**
How others see us and how we see ourselves according to factors such as birth, income, education, lifestyle. (Rich, Poor, Middle Class, High-School or University-Educated, etc.)

☐ **Physiology and Physical Limitations**
How body size and shape, structural or functional differences, or limits to physical or mental abilities affect our self-perception and others' perception of us. (Tall, Short, Heavy, Thin, Disfigured, Deaf, Paraplegic, etc.)

With these distinctions fresh in your mind, next time you read a newspaper or listen to a news broadcast, notice how many of the stories involve cultural background, (either directly or just below the surface). See if you also notice, how, when reading or listening, you tend to judge others because of their race, gender, social class, occupation, nationality, physical make-up, sexual preference, age, philosophy or where they live.

WHY PEOPLE ANSWER QUESTIONS DIFFERENTLY

Culture lives in our language. Certainly the native language that people speak shows the culture they come from. But culture also lives in how we spontaneously talk to ourselves both consciously and unconsciously. Culture determines whether our communication has more emphasis on words, pictures, sounds, or feelings. It is always with us whether we are aware of it or not.

Every time we see or hear something or someone, we instantly begin to talk to ourselves. Our mind races to answer two questions:

What does this mean?
What should I do about it?

To answer each question, we look in our ''library'' or ''data base.'' This is drawn from what living in our culture has taught us. We have opinions about everything—without even trying! Culture is always talking to us.

More than 2000 years ago, philosophers identified four basic judgments which we automatically make in order to figure out what is happening and what to do about it:

1. **Is it ONE or MANY?**
2. **Is it TRUE or FALSE?**
3. **Is it GOOD or EVIL?**
4. **Is it BEAUTIFUL or UGLY?**

These are called TRANSCENDENTAL QUESTIONS because:

• They are found in all cultures and languages. Every thinking human being asks these questions automatically.

• They go beyond any single subject. We apply them instinctively to everything we discuss with ourselves and each other.

EXERCISE: YOUR MIND AT WORK

Let's see how your "culture" shows up when your mind reacts to some words.

Look at the words and phrases in the list below. A "conversation" should start in your mind. Describe briefly in the first empty column the picture, words, or scene your mind spontaneously gave you.

In the second column, jot down any automatic judgments your mind made, e.g. true/false, good/bad, beautiful/ugly. You really *do* have an opinion about everything.

Finally, in the remaining column, write down where you first experienced your idea or feeling. Identify the source of your attitude if possible.

Remember, notice what your automatic mind and your culture say. You are neither good nor bad because of it. It is what you do with it later that counts. Two different people for example could come up with quite different answers as the examples for "immigrant" show.

WORD	WHAT I GOT	JUDGMENTS	SOURCE
immigrant or immigrant	picture of person on a boat an unshaven worker	good, brave bad, they scare me	my grandmother's stories my dad avoided them
money			
home			
foreigners			
management			
working woman			
artist			
death penalty			
white men			
unions			
gay or lesbian			
college			
marriage			
work			

WHO INFLUENCES YOU?

Because of what we experience in acquiring our cultural background, we do not all have the same answers to the questions our minds ask. Our minds do not work in the same way.

> *Grover believes the death penalty keeps people from committing crimes—he grew up in a lawless environment where people felt very angry and vengeful about the threats to their well-being. Karin disapproves and believes it incites violence—she comes from a country with little or no violence and no death penalty.*
>
> *Nikki, whose mother was a lawyer, finds it good that women work outside the home—she says it enriches them. Fran was educated to be a homemaker and a mother. She thinks jobs for women are bad because they tend to make women less feminine.*
>
> *Why does Gila admire abstract art, while Leroy detests it? Why does Dimitri like Chinese food while Maria can't stomach it?*

Our minds are anchored in the past. While this helps us make sense of things, it can also keep us from understanding and working with each other. Complete the exercise below:

Many people influenced our attitudes about others when we were young. Think back to when you grew up. Who were some people whose words and actions made you fear, suspect, or avoid people who were different from you? What did they say and do? Which people reinforce the same feelings now? Make a list of things you learned from these people that you would like to avoid or change now.

_____

_____

_____

_____

Who were the people during your youth who helped you be open to others? What do they say and do? Jot down some of the things that you would like to imitate or initiate.

_____

_____

_____

_____

TRANSCENDENTAL QUESTION: ONE OR MANY?

One question our mind asks, ''Is it one or many?'' is not easy to grasp. But it is very important when working with people who are different from us. Here are some examples of how we make or fail to make distinctions about *what belongs together and what doesn't* or about *what's the same and what's different.*

When we look at something through the eyes of our culture or experience, we have more names for it because we have more uses for it:

- *Harvey lives in a big city. For him all snow is the same—pretty to look at, but a nuisance to drive in.*

- *Moira, who lives next door to Harvey, is a skier. She divides ''snow'' into ''popcorn,'' ''powder,'' ''mashed potatoes'' or ''ice,'' and knows how to ski on each type.*

- *Inuk, a Native American who lives in the Yukon, sees ''snow'' as more than twenty different things and has a word and a use for each.*

Because of our background, we see some things in more detail than others:

- *For Lucia, the computer is simply a tool to do accounting.*

- *Balbir, an electrical engineer, sees a computer as a complex device made up of many interrelating parts.*

The same is true about how we look at people:

- *Sukirno, a postal worker who lives in Sumatra, sees Indonesians as more than 300 different peoples.*

- *Jane, who works in a department store in London, thinks all ''Asians'' look and act the same.*

By asking, ''Is it one or many?'' our minds try to decide what fits together and what doesn't. When we answer it, *we either include or exclude others from a group according to our cultural standards and experience.* We not only separate ''us'' from ''them,'' but we decide how we are alike and how we are different.

We can choose to live in separate worlds because of how we think, or we can learn to see people in all their richness and appreciate their differences. We can look at them as individuals *as well* as representatives of different cultures. We can also see how we all belong to the larger human family. When it comes to people, it is important to see both sides of how we are one and how we are many!

PREJUDICE—WE ALL HAVE IT

If you look only from the center of your personal or cultural "solar system" your mind will automatically conclude that:

The world consists of "us" and "them."
We are right, they are wrong.
We are good, they are bad.
We are beautiful, they are ugly.

As a result it is not uncommon in history to find groups persecuting others. History shows one culture viewing another as sub-human, morally inferior, technologically backward, or not having "true" faith. Less severe but common prejudice appears when culture rejects another on the basis of, "I wouldn't want my sister to marry one," or, "Some of my best friends are: _____, but..."

> Learning how our minds prejudge others is a first step in managing our minds.

SUBJECTIVE → OBJECTIVE

We often make facts out of our opinions, feelings, and preferences when we talk about them. We say things like, "The sales group is too noisy," rather than, "I'm having difficulty concentrating when so many people are talking at once." Or, "Arabs are too pushy," rather than, "I get uncomfortable when Hakim speaks and gestures so close to me."

In other words, prejudice can get started when we make our own interpretation of what we experience (something *subjective*), into an absolute truth about others (something *objective*), which we then believe ourselves and spread to other people.

REVERSING THE PROCESS

Let's practice reversing the process of converting subjective experiences into objective statements. Convert the sentences below from objective to subjective statements. Do this by changing the statements about groups to statements about one individual's feelings toward others.

Women are too emotional. _____

_____

Americans are too individualistic. _____

_____

Hispanics stick to themselves too much. _____

_____

What things do you say about other groups? Change the two such statements below into statements about yourself.

1. *What I say about them:* _____

_____

   What I'm actually saying about me: _____

_____

2. *What I say about them:* _____

_____

   What I'm actually saying about me: _____

_____

> Thinking and talking about our experience in subjective terms will keep us from creating prejudices about people as groups.

CONFIRMATION BIAS: RESISTING NEW INFORMATION ABOUT OTHERS

Our minds have what psychologists call a *confirmation bias*. We try to fit new information into old categories, to make what we learn agree with what we already know. We tend to warp incoming data and ignore information that doesn't agree with what we *think* we already know.

If we feel, for example, that people of a certain background are usually late, we focus on their tardiness and call them "lazy" *as a group* while ignoring other individuals who may do the same thing. If we believe people of a certain culture are stingy or greedy, we will always be looking for them to act that way and ignore when they are giving. What we believe of them becomes "true," simply because we believe it.

> Prejudice is a self-fulfilling prophecy! Our minds have a "place" for certain kinds of people, and work hard to keep them there.

FILLING IN THE BLANKS

Our minds also like to *fill in the blanks.* Maybe that's why some people like puzzles so much, or why as children we enjoyed gazing at the stars or the clouds and making pictures and stories out of them.

Look at the symbols drawn below and watch how your mind tries "fill in the blanks" to make sense out of them.

Write whatever message you think each symbol contains in the space provided. Then turn the page over to find out what the symbols actually say.

_____

_____

_____

_____

Bob Abramms-Mezoff of ODT, Inc. has observed how our tendency to fill in the blanks produces the "halo effect." We assume that people who are good at one thing will be good at something else. For example, that an accountant will manage his or her personal finances well, or that a kind and indulgent manager will be a good "family person." And the reverse—which is even more damaging—that a person who is poor at one thing will be poor at something else. For example, that a factory worker who speaks poorly will not understand machines either.

Sometimes we even go beyond the "halo effect" to infer that a person of a different culture who fails at a part of his or her job is simply inferior and will not succeed at anything. All of these are symptoms of "filling in the blanks."

> This line of characters has no message. It is composed of random symbols. They were put here to allow you to see how your mind uses its cultural "data base", i.e. what you already know to interpret whatever it encounters.

FILLING IN THE BLANKS (Continued)

When we catch our minds "filling in the blanks" we need to remind ourselves how little we know about others and then try to find out more.

What is prejudice? Some very normal mental functions are the source of what we call *prejudice*. Our minds "pre-judge" things. It is unavoidable. *Pre-judging is something our minds absolutely must do.* Without prejudging, we would have so many decisions to make we would be unable to cope with life.

In many matters, we can afford to be a little bit wrong and still come out okay. When it comes to other people, however, our minds often have false information, or we simply don't know enough to make good judgments. Our prejudice can make us wrong because it can cause us to be unfair if we act on it without looking for more information or asking for a second opinion.

It is not our fault that we have prejudices, however, it is our fault if we allow them to run our lives and tear down the lives of others. In the end, people with prejudices are the real losers. Their lives become narrow and mean and they miss out on new ideas and fresh ways of looking at things. When rejecting or despising others, we are usually rejecting or despising parts of ourselves. Parts we have been afraid to acknowledge. We often "put down" others because we think so little of ourselves that we try to make others smaller so we can look bigger. This keeps us small. Prejudice is a double-edged sword and the sharper edge is the one we use to cut ourselves.

Write something you missed out on because you judged someone unfairly or too quickly.

MY MISSED OPPORTUNITY

HOW TO MANAGE CULTURAL DISCOMFORT

Our cultural differences show up in how we "talk" to ourselves about ourselves and about others. This is not just an intellectual problem. Much of it takes place in what Minninger and Dugan call the "silent mind." The silent mind works below the level of our awareness and causes us to react automatically or habitually with feelings and sometimes with actions. This happens, for example, when people who are different from us appear or do something which makes their differences stand out. Look at the following examples and imagine of how you might be affected in a similar situation.

> *Lee Ming is embarrassed when she must talk to Lester, a subordinate who lost an arm. She does not know how to look at him or how to talk about his limitation. As a result, she rushes the meeting and avoids giving Lester bad news that she fears he might find hard to take.*

Things I think, feel, or ways I react to someone who is disfigured or disabled or ill:

_____

_____

_____

> *Hans feels afraid when negotiating with his supervisor Henry. Henry is a much larger man than Hans and is from a different racial background. When talking to Hans he seems to stare. Hans finds himself avoiding Henry except when absolutely necessary.*

My reaction to someone of a different race:

_____

_____

_____

HOW TO MANAGE CULTURAL DISCOMFORT (Continued)

Hector is a personnel officer. Whenever a beautiful woman walks in for an interview, he automatically puts on his ''charming gentleman act.'' He finds later that he has not paid attention to parts of the interview and his report is inaccurate. The woman doesn't get hired, or gets hired for the wrong job.

How I respond to someone of the opposite sex:

_____

_____

Kalid becomes angry when several of the people he works with chatter among themselves in their native language. He suspects they are talking and laughing about him or just wasting time. He finds himself being irritable with them, avoiding them and complains about them to others.

How I react to people who speak a different language around me:

_____

_____

Juanita is charmed by Luc's French accent on the telephone. Even though they have never met and their dealings are strictly business, she spends much more time on Luc's reports than she does on those of the other overseas agents.

How other accents affect me:

_____

_____

YOUR "COMFORT ZONES": AN EXERCISE

The following worksheet will help you see how contacts with different people might make you uncomfortable, cause stress, leave you less effective, or lead you to act unfairly. If you have difficulty thinking of situations, ask others who observe you and whom you know will be honest with you.

With whom or what type of person am I uncomfortable or disturbed by in some way?

_____

When dealing with others, in what kind of situation does their being different cause me to react?

_____

What reactions do I have? What do I say to myself? How do I feel?

_____

_____

_____

On a scale of one to five, how much does this disable or hinder me from dealing effectively with issues or from giving this person fair treatment?

1 = minor—by becoming aware of it, I can usually put it aside,

5 = major—the situation seems to take over and I don't feel like I have any control over it or skills to deal with it.

1———2———3———4———5

How might I make a change? Who might be able to give me information, feedback or support in improving my performance?

_____

_____

_____

_____

Return to this page and make further notes as you continue to learn more about managing cultural diversity. Feel free to photocopy this page to work on other situations for yourself.

TRANSCENDENTAL QUESTION: GOOD & BEAUTIFUL VS. BAD & UGLY?

Keep in mind that some kind of comfort or discomfort will always be present when we interact with someone of a different culture. The trick is to not allow ourselves to play favorites or treat others unfairly. Also, we can't assume that other people feel about us as we feel about them, though we often "fill in the blanks" this way.

Did you ever look into a kaleidoscope? The bits of glass fall into infinitely diverse patterns. Having nothing to win or lose by looking into the kaleidoscope, we can let ourselves relax and be fascinated by the beauty of the designs we see.

Occasionally we see the goodness and beauty of human diversity in the same way. For example, leafing through a travel brochure or the pages of *National Geographic,* or watching a human interest video about a culture different from our own.

What are some things you have admired at a distance about people who differ from yourself? Write your responses below:

_____

_____

_____

_____

GOOD & BEAUTIFUL VS.
BAD & UGLY (Continued)

Our everyday experience with others is not so simple. We are often annoyed by people's differences or annoy them with ours. "Rubbing each other the wrong way," we develop sore spots and pet peeves. When this happens, we decide not to work with or hire another on the basis of, "I'm just not comfortable with so-and-so." We keep our resources or information for those we are comfortable with and deal with others as *bad and ugly.* As a result, cultural differences almost always lead us to make "insiders" and "outsiders", and to act unfairly to "outsiders."

We divide people into "haves" and "have nots." The "have nots" are a threat to what we have, while the "haves" are a force to "keep us in our place." Take a look at the map of the world or at who holds which jobs or gets which benefits in your community or workplace. You will quickly see how race, sex and other cultural differences divide us economically and socially. They are more than just "interesting" differences to look at.

Take a few moments to recognize some of the economic and social *dividing lines* in your workplace or community. Identify the *cultural difference* on which the distinction is based in the space provided below.

Dividing line	Cultural difference
Example: *In my workplace almost all the lower level support staff jobs are held by women.*	*Gender-male vs. female*
(Add your examples)	

It is hard to get people to do something about the everyday realities of social injustice, or the violence and crime created by both poverty and wealth. Comfortable people are reluctant to disturb their comfort and it is hard for those who are hurting to look beyond their pain. Fear often causes us to treat others unfairly and keeps us from the urgent task of building a better world and a better workplace together.

TURN FEAR INTO CURIOSITY

Managing the mind means turning fear into curiosity about what could be. Curiosity can lead to new possibilities. Curiosity and excitement are the "flip side" of fear and anxiety. Two people can stand side by side in line to ride a roller coaster and have the same sweaty palms and churning stomach, yet one says, "I'm excited," and the other says, "I'm terrified." Some people are stimulated by the opportunity to move into a new job, others are frightened. How can we get from fear to excitement?

Because curiosity is fed by the same energy as fear, we can move from one emotion to the other more easily than we think. We do this by changing how we talk to ourselves about what is going on. The best way to succeed is to picture "What if...?" What if we could get beyond our differences? Use the image below to note some of your fears about other people on the shadowy side of the door and on the bright side turn them into possibilities by envisioning what if...?

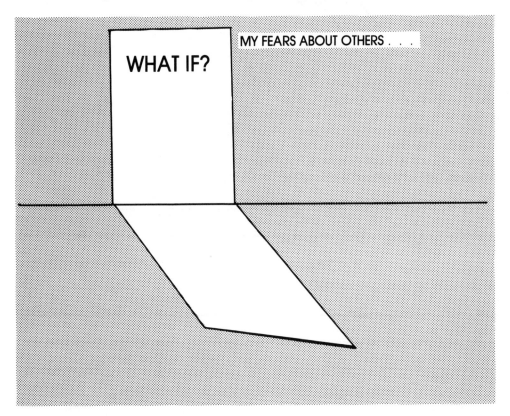

CHECK YOUR PROGRESS

What have been some "eye-openers" or important things you have learned from this book thus far? List them in the space provided below:

_____

_____

_____

_____

_____

_____

Turn back to page iv and review the goals you set for yourself there. At this point in the book, how would you change or add to what you would like to get out of this workbook.

SECTION TWO
MANAGE YOUR WORDS

We've evaluated how we ''talk to ourselves.'' Now it's time to examine how we talk to and about each other. Learning how to use words carefully can improve how we work together.

In this section, we will investigate name-calling and humor, two trouble spots in a multicultural environment. We will learn a technique which will help us remain sensitive to each others' feelings. We will find out what to do when people who work together speak different languages.

Because people in different cultures think and talk differently, there will be tips on how to clear up misunderstandings and make agreements that work. Finally, we will look at politics, the way groups talk to each other to achieve important goals.

NAME-CALLING

Spoken words reflect our minds. They have a great impact on how we get along with, or don't get along with, each other. In this section, we will look at words as the primary tools with which we try to understand each other and create agreements between us that work. Because we use words to name things and describe each other as groups, let's look at that first.

Naming Cultural Groups

Some of the names which people give to cultural groups are disrespectful, (or have become so over time.)

What are some names given to cultural groups to which you belong? Which of these are uncomfortable for you and which are o.k.?

NAME	NOT O.K.	O.K.
Example: "Girl"	☑	☐

ADD YOUR OWN:

	NOT O.K.	O.K.
_____	☐	☐
_____	☐	☐
_____	☐	☐
_____	☐	☐
_____	☐	☐

People sometimes use inappropriate names for other groups out of ignorance. They either don't know the proper name or don't understand how sensitive others are to certain names. Some people demean others because they think so little of themselves. Putting others down makes them feel better or more important.

If someone you know calls others by a disrespectful name, speak up. Tell them how you feel. If possible tell them in a way that will help them to make a change without putting them down or blaming them. Make sure you let them know how you would like your group to be called.

Sometimes we tend to get a little too "thickskinned" for our own good. We grow to accept names that are demeaning to ourselves and the cultural group we belong to. We allow ourselves to be called a "girl" or "kid" or tolerate a racial or ethnic nickname that is unflattering. Letting others push us around has the same root as name-calling, low self-esteem. In this case we don't think enough of ourselves to insist on a change.

NAME-CALLING (Continued)

Review the list you made on page 26 and circle any inappropriate names you have come to accept.

What names are used for other cultural groups where you live and work? Are these names acceptable to the people to whom they refer? What are the right terms? If you don't know, ask! Using the space below find correct names for the groups of the people you work with and speak about.

NAMES USED	APPROPRIATE NAME

If you have called someone by an inappropriate name either inadvertently or in a time of stress or anger, don't defend your mistake or give excuses—*just apologize!* Then find a way to remind yourself so you don't repeat the same mistake.

RESPECTING PERSONAL NAMES

Individuals have the right to say how they want to be called. It is up to you to find out and use words to describe people acceptable to them. This especially goes for people's personal names. Here is a checklist that will help you. Mark those boxes you promise to follow:

☐ I will learn to pronounce the name correctly, (i.e. as they do.)

☐ I will learn how people are addressed in their own language and the right time to use a family name or a given name.

☐ I will be sensitive to the fact that in certain cultures, the order in which one writes or speaks the family and given names may be different from my own. Some cultures give many names, some few or even a single one.

☐ I will learn the titles of respect that go with other's names and when it is appropriate to use them.

☐ I will call people by their proper name. I will avoid the use of slang names, such as ''Honey,'' ''Dear,'' ''Babe,'' ''Mama,'' ''Sweetheart,'' ''Fella,'' ''Guy,'' ''Mac,'' ''Ace'' etc. which annoy most people.

USING HUMOR APPROPRIATELY

Humor is one of our greatest human assets. It helps us withdraw from tense situations and enables us to come back to resolve them with a relaxed or fresh point of view.

Humor, in the form of irony, satire, ridicule, or stereotyping, is also one of the most socially destructive weapons available. Think of some of the devastating political cartoons you have seen in newspapers.

The secret to good humor lies in whether we are laughing with people or at them. Following are some simple hints about using humor in multicultural situations.

LAUGHING WITH EACH OTHER
Life is full of funny events and touching moments. Being able to laugh at ourselves and our predicaments endears us to each other. The best story is one you can tell about yourself or about your experiences in such a way that others can recognize themselves in you and you can laugh together.

Multicultural situations will get you into many laughable scenes. Just remember the first time you tried something that was foreign to you, for example, the first time you used chopsticks or silverware, or used a bathroom in a strange culture, or showed up in the wrong place at the wrong time! Look for chances to laugh at yourself, and others will laugh with you. Knowing how to laugh at yourself helps you see that your own cultural outlook is only one of many ways to see the world.

LAUGHING AT EACH OTHER
Don't tell ethnic jokes—ever. Or stories that make fun of peoples' cultures. Almost all of these jokes are built on making some group of people seem inferior. They exaggerate stereotypes of how people look and act. Even ethnic jokes about your own cultural group may create hard feelings.

Sexual humor, more often than not, degrades both women and men. In addition, just talking about sex itself may offend some people.

Telling ethnic or sexual jokes is like name-calling. It is frequently used to bond a group to keep outsiders in their place. It may seem to make us feel good about ourselves while we are doing it, but unconsciously it reinforces stereotypes and our negative views of others.

USING HUMOR APPROPRIATELY
(Continued)

In multicultural environments, and in times of change, group sensibilities run high. Unless you're confident that the jokes you tell and how you tell them won't offend any group at all, you should refrain from joke telling in general!

How would you handle a joke told by someone else that was unfair to you or to another cultural group? Check the approach you feel you would use. Would you:

1. Go on as if it had not taken place, but later take the person aside and alert them to your feelings on the matter.

2. Denounce the storyteller in public.

3. Tell an appropriate joke as a model for the kind of jokes that should be told.

4. Laugh now but tell the person about your discomfort later in private.

5. Tell an even worse joke about the other person's group.

GUIDELINES

Some guidelines for evaluating your choices are presented in the upside down box at the bottom of this page. Compare your response with the author's comments in the box.

1. Perhaps the best overall strategy. It sends a message of disapproval without creating a disruptive conflict.

2. If the stakes are high enough, or the person doesn't get the message of silence, you may want to do this and face the conflict. Using the "Ouch!" method (see page 31) is a good middle road between 1 and 2, but people need to know about it beforehand.

3. A poor strategy. People probably won't get the message. They may simply hear you giving them permission to continue with more of the same.

4. Pulling the person aside later may be a benefit to both them and the group insulted, especially, as is often the case, when the person was ignorant or insensitive rather than malicious. Laughing, however, may encourage the storytelling to continue.

5. May lead to a fierce game of "Can you top this?" Not recommended as a strategy to promote understanding.

USING HUMOR APPROPRIATELY
(Continued)

TEASING

Teasing takes place when we use a little bit of aggression to show affection for another person. As with joke telling, it is important to avoid ethnic and cultural issues.

Some teasing consists of rather strong ''ragging'' or put-downs. This is often done by men. They trade insults! This way of saying they like each other may be totally misunderstood by women and certain other cultural groups.

Rita Risser, author of *How to Work with Men*, suggests a four-step strategy to use if you find yourself a victim in the ''Insult Game.''

- First, recognize that it is a game.
- Second, observe carefully until you know the rules of the game.
- Third, sharpen your wits and play along.
- Finally, accompany your jab with a smile.

Her advice will probably work for the ways this game is played in most cultures. Wherever you are, making sure you know the rules (step two) is the most important.

JUST LIKE A MAN!

Women have always made fun of men. Today more than ever, as a result of changing consciousness of women and minorities in much of the world, many people are angry with traditional male dominance in certain aspects of society. Frustration with this system, (in which men as well as women and other minorities have been caught), sometimes turns into hostility toward the male gender. This surfaces in sarcastic humor, ridiculous stereotypes, and cutting remarks about men as men. If you are a man, here are some ways to deal with the situation:

- Recognize that you personally have not created the system in which women and men find themselves today.
- Laugh at yourself when you do fall into one of the male stereotypes.
- Put yourself in the shoes of women and minorities. Listen carefully to hear the frustration and the real needs behind the sarcasm and wisecracks.
- Use what power you have to change things that are unfair.
- Don't expect a lot of sympathy for male dilemmas. Your best understanding and support will come from other men who are beginning to have an awareness of the problems of cultural and gender diversity.

THE "OUCH!" TECHNIQUE

Following is a trick you can use to help a multicultural organization, team or group become more aware of each other's cultural sensibilities and sore spots. Get the people in your group to agree to call out the simple word, "Ouch!" when someone in the group says or does something which offends them or makes them uncomfortable.

It works for inappropriate humor or offensive jokes as well as for other things which people say or do which insult or hurt someone of another background.

It's like getting your toe stepped on. Most of the time people don't stomp on your feet intentionally. When you say, "Ouch!", they get off right away, say, "I'm sorry," and are more careful where they step the next time. "Ouch," is all the feedback people normally need.

Unless what has been said or done is so painful that it keeps the group from continuing, or the purpose of the group is to explore tension between cultures, don't stop to discuss the incident. Getting deeply into feelings and sensibilities when you have another agenda can turn into attacking, defending, or deciding who's right or wrong instead of accomplishing the task at hand.

Saying, "Ouch!" whenever something hurts quickly helps us to know and respect each other's cultural and personal boundaries.

Think of a common situation that is an "Ouch!" for you and jot it down in a few words on the blank lines in the illustration above.

HOW TO BRIDGE THE LANGUAGE BARRIER

WHEN WE DON'T SPEAK THE SAME LANGUAGE

It is almost always easier for us to speak our mother tongue than someone else's language. Unless we learned more than one language as a child, it is rare for us to be fully fluent in a second tongue. In some countries, like the U.S. and Australia, it is rare for people (who are not recent immigrants), to master more than one language.

Education, training, and experience also give us "different" languages. Software engineers speak "computerese," attorneys speak "legalese," and construction workers talk "hardhat!"

When people are speaking different languages (or using unfamiliar jargon) in the same place, it can easily cause misunderstandings and hard feelings. Here are some ways to avoid this situation. Rate your ability to use them on the scales below:

HOW I BRIDGE THE LANGUAGE BARRIER

1) I learn and use the language or jargon of the dominant culture in which I find myself at the moment.

1	2	3	4	5
can't do		am learning		do regularly

> *Tip:* *When you are a visitor where people do not speak your language, start immediately by learning some of the simpler phrases for everyday interactions. Knowing how to say, "Hello," "Goodbye," "Please," "Thank you," etc. can go a long way toward creating respect and good will. But, don't stop there!*
>
> *Being forced to learn the dominant language has sometimes been a way of oppressing minorities. Choosing to learn someone else's language doesn't mean you have to give up your own or value it less.*

2) If I must speak to someone in a language that others in the same conversation or nearby don't understand, I interpret for them or ask someone to interpret for me.

1	2	3	4	5
can't do		am learning		do regularly

> *Tip:* *If the conversation seems too unimportant to relate word for word, stop from time to time to inform others of the gist of what you are discussing in your language.*

HOW TO BRIDGE THE LANGUAGE BARRIER (Continued)

3) Instead of becoming impatient and judging others as less intelligent, I make allowances for those who speak the language less fluently.

1	2	3	4	5
can't do		am learning		do regularly

> *Tip: Besides being patient, it will help to speak more slowly, use simple words, and avoid slang. It is usually not helpful to try to imitate the other person's limited use of the language, (e.g. by speaking "broken English"). It is particularly offensive to raise your voice and speak louder, as if the other person were hard of hearing, when they simply cannot understand your words or your accent.*
>
> *Realize that thinking in and speaking a foreign language can be as fatiguing as hard physical work. It is important to notice when people are beginning to tire and provide breaks. If you are speaking someone else's tongue, be sure to tell them when they are going too fast or when you are beginning to "fade."*

4) If one of us is less familiar with the language, I listen carefully and check back from time to time to make sure each of us understands what the other is saying.

1	2	3	4	5
can't do		am learning		do regularly

> *Tip: Simply repeating back in your own words what you heard, or asking the other person, "Could you tell me how you understand what we have said so far?", will help you check on how well you are getting across to each other. To improve your listening skills, consider ordering* The Business of Listening *using the form in the back of this book.*

WHEN WE SPEAK THE SAME LANGUAGE

How people speak; their accents, the words they choose, their rhythm and pace, if different from ours, may automatically bring a positive or negative judgment from our minds. For example:

• We may find accents charming, mysterious, annoying, or simply difficult to understand.

Lloyd finds Judith's flat Chicago accent makes her plain and boorish, while Judith thinks Lloyd's Oxford English makes him more intelligent than Chen, the chief engineer, whose Hong Kong English seems sing-songy and childish to her. Once they get to know each other, they discover that none of these judgments are valid.

• They may sound too haughty or too subservient.

Raj learned to use formal and indirect language when speaking to persons in authority. His new boss thinks that Raj lacks conviction about his own ideas and is afraid to make decisions.

• The pacing and timing may be different.

Shiela is from New York City, where people normally talk over the ends of each others sentences and find it stimulating. Jimmy is from Iowa where people pause slightly after another has finished before starting to speak. When Shiela speaks to Jimmy, she finds him dull. Jimmy thinks Shiela is rude.

Tip: *Remember once again that the judgments we make are usually just our culture talking. Be fair to others!*

When entering a conversation, try to match the pace and timing of the people with whom you are speaking. This may actually establish more rapport than what you have to say to them. Excellent salespersons often do this. They take their cues from their client and match the ebb and flow of the client's speech.

Sometimes people learn a second language by reading and studying rather than conversing with native speakers. They are able to compose what they want to say, but still are not understood well or fail to understand others well because of accent and pacing. If this is a hinderance for you or people you work with, look into taking or providing a course in accent reduction. Accents add variety to our conversations and are part of our personality, so don't feel they should be suppressed. We just need to work with them a bit if intelligibility is a major problem.

In a sentence, describe the characteristics of your own accent. If you need help, ask someone different from you for feedback:

_____

_____

BE CLEAR TO OTHERS

Within a culture, many things are understood without having to be spoken. People understand what time to arrive for a meeting or for dinner. They know who speaks to whom and who doesn't. They are aware of things to chat about and things too personal to informally discuss. However, when cultures mix, strange things happen.

PLEASE BATHE ONLY WITHIN THE BATHTUB AS THE BATHROOM FLOOR HAS NO DRAIN.

Western visitors to Malaysia, for example, are usually humored to find a sign like the one above in bathrooms of Western style hotels. They assume that everyone knows how to bathe in a bathtub and prefers to do so. Little do they realize that some cultures normally bathe outside a water tub by pouring water over themselves and would find bathing inside the tub unsanitary and odd.

When people from different cultures mix, such as when large numbers of immigrants enter a country or move into a new neighborhood, common understanding is often weakened. When diverse groups are brought together in the work force or in a multinational corporation, we can no longer assume that everybody has the same unspoken mental language. We can't "read between the lines" any more.

Newcomers don't know the unwritten rules of the culture they enter, and oldtimers don't realize that the newcomers bring different ones with them until something goes wrong, or someone is embarrassed. Think of your first day on a new job, and the worries and questions you had about where things were and how things were done. Entering another culture is ten times harder. This means that for a long while, almost everything has to be spelled out word for word and lots of questions need to be encouraged and answered.

LEARNING NEW RULES

When enough newcomers enter a neighborhood or organization, it is common for both sides to be uncomfortable. People get annoyed with the "others" because they are used to having people of their own culture understand them without having to be so explicit. On the other hand, when told things explicitly by "others," they may find it "pushy" or impolite, or feel they are treated like children. On both sides people fail to define what they need, want or mean. When this occurs, they are disappointed and upset because others fail to understand what to do.

Think of experiences you have had working with people from another culture. What were some of the things that were difficult, uncomfortable or embarrassing for you to have to tell them?

_____

_____

_____

Take a similar experience when you were really on someone else's cultural "turf." What were a few of the things which others felt you should have understood and were surprised or shocked or humored to find out that you didn't?

_____

_____

_____

Remember that for all practical purposes, *the meaning of anything you say is what the other person understands*. It doesn't matter what you intended to say, their response tells you the message they got. If the other person is not clearly responding in the way you want them to, you must *do something else* to get the message across. Becoming frustrated, angry, or blaming wastes time and creates hard feelings. Most of the time people do their best to understand each other.

THE BASICS OF COMMUNICATING

Fortunately, despite the hundreds of languages and cultures, people only do selected things with language. Fernando Flores, President of Logonet, an education technology company, and coauthor of *Understanding Computers and Cognition*, summarized the most important speech acts which we perform. These include:

FOUR BASIC SPEECH ACTS

1. We ask others to do things.

> Examples: I ask you to finish the budget by Friday noon.
> I insist that you stay for the whole meeting.
> Please give me ten minutes.

2. We promise others that we will do things (or refuse).

> Examples: I promise to meet you at the cafeteria at 7:00 tomorrow morning.
> Yes, if you come to the shop tomorrow, I assure you, I'll be there.
> No, I will not consider this part of my job.

3. We assert that certain things are true or false.

> Examples: All the seats on this flight have been taken.
> This metal part will not wear as well as a nylon one.
> I have evidence to show that we are losing sales in this market.

4. We declare or define an objective or goal, state an attitude we are going to have, or, proclaim a new state of affairs. In effect, we say to others, ''This is how it's going to be from now on.'' We do this on the basis of our right to manage our own lives or on the authority others have given us to get a job done.

> Examples: Anyone who smokes within the posted area will be reprimanded.
> I apologize for neglecting to inform you as I promised.
> Thank you for reminding me.
> You're hired! You will supervise the team.
> I'm going to become a salesperson.

THE BASICS OF COMMUNICATING
(Continued)

CHECK IT OUT

At the end of your next meeting see which of the four speech acts have come into play. Ask yourself:

☐ Have I asked something of the other person or they of me?

☐ Have I promised something to them or they to me?

☐ Were we telling each other about what is true and false?

☐ Were either of us committing ourselves to a new attitude, direction, definition or state of affairs?

Keep these four questions in mind to use as a checklist. If you can answer them fully when you complete a business transaction, or had a conversation about work with a co-worker of a different culture, you will know what you have agreed upon, no matter how indirect, "chatty" or polite the conversation seemed.

This is not to say that "how" we deal with others is less important than what we agree on. If we don't pay attention to the "how," we may get no agreement at all!

CULTURAL DOUBLE BINDS

Certain cross-cultural situations are hard to manage because they seem to put us in a no-win position. Following are some ''double binds'' with tips about how to handle them.

1. SAYING ''NO''

> *Wolf managed a team of Asian engineers in an overseas installation for his company. He laid out a project plan and explained it to the group. No one disagreed and they started to work. Four days into the project, Mori, one of the engineers, failed to produce the needed data for a critical part of the plan. Wolf was angry at Mori who promised to do his best. A few minutes later Wolf spoke to a supervisor who told him that Mori has been in the computer room past midnight each night for the last four days.*

In many cultures saying ''No'' to someone's request or offer even if it seems unreasonable is taboo. The person who does not agree usually sends other signals that indicate something is wrong. These may be too subtle to detect if you are not from that culture.

In other cultures, ''No'' is never said to one in authority. This may also be true of subcultures within a larger culture. Sometimes women have allowed less power to say ''No'' than men. Certain functions within an organization may have difficulty with it. Again, usually other signals are sent. The untrained outsider who misses the signals may feel that an agreement has taken place and be surprised when what ''was promised'' never shows up.

In yet other cultures, saying ''No'' is simply a signal to renegotiate a better agreement. This may seem very discourteous, even dangerous to people of the first two kinds of cultures.

> *Tips:* *You need to get specific information about how disagreement is handled in the other person's culture.*
>
> *When dealing with people who are reluctant to say ''No,'' check the agreements you think you have made more than once, and look for any signs of discomfort before going ahead.*
>
> *When dealing with someone who expects a ''yes'' or ''no'' and such directness is uncomfortable for you, begin in low-risk situations and get feedback from someone in the culture who will tell you how you sound. When learning how to communicate in another culture, we often miss nuances and overdo it. Feedback can help us ''fine tune'' our performance.*

Check the box below that describes the degree to which saying ''No'' might be a problem between you and those of other cultures. Then jot down the strategy you would use to deal with it.

SAYING ''NO''

☐ is not an issue   ☐ may be an issue   ☐ certainly is an issue

My strategy for dealing with ''saying no'' is: _____

CULTURAL DOUBLE BINDS
(Continued)

2. POLITENESS VS. DIRECTNESS

> *Jeanne is conducting a technical training program for a multicultural group of assemblers in a Vancouver hi-tech production facility. Most who took her course gave her excellent ratings. She was feeling very good about her performance until several of the trainees asked her to demonstrate the basic procedures again.*

In some cultures people find it impolite to complain or to say that they don't understand something. To do so in their own culture would be to cause the other person to "lose face." So, problems are either subtly and indirectly communicated, or a third person is used as a go-between to carry the feedback or "bad news."

More direct cultures may judge this as underhanded, cowardly, or a waste of time. These people "lay their cards on the table" the moment a problem or disagreement arises. People from the indirect culture may find this uncivilized, disrespectful, or deliberately insulting. Sharing feelings too openly may look like insincerity to them.

> *Tips:* *Learn about the other person's culture. What do people in that culture tend to talk about and what do they tend to hold back?*
>
> *Find an informant, someone who knows both cultures well enough to explain them.*
>
> *Be cautious with criticism until you know how to give it.*
>
> *If giving criticism is hard for you but expected by others, learn that criticizing facts or results is not a criticism of the person. Point out what is correct or working and then show how other parts could be improved.*

Check the box below that describes how much of a problem politeness or directness might be for you and others with whom you live or work. Then, using what you know so far and the tips given here, jot down the strategy you would use to deal with it.

Politeness vs. Directness

☐ is not an issue   ☐ may be an issue   ☐ certainly is an issue

My strategy for dealing with it is _____

_____

_____

CULTURAL DOUBLE BINDS
(Continued)

3. PRIMITIVE BEHAVIOR & POLARIZATION UNDER PRESSURE

> *A task force has been formed to develop a strategic plan for organizing the company around a new product line. The task force includes participants from every level in the organization and is to be a model for a new open attitude towards diversity in the company. As the deadline approaches, the senior managers, start making decisions on their own without consulting the junior members. When the junior members complain about this, they are labelled "young radicals" and told that they are poor team players. The junior members start holding caucuses of their own to deal with what they claim is dishonesty on the part of senior managers.*

In times of stress or pressure, people tend to revert to earlier behaviors. They act in ways that are most typical of their culture and deal with others in primitive stereotypes. They tend to polarize into opposing groups and exert power and pressure against each other. They deal with issues on a political rather than a personal level. They blame people who are different for everything that is going wrong. Name calling may occur.

> *Tip: First, prevent taking sides as much as possible. It is extremely important in culturally diverse populations, groups, and organizations to continually strive to work at the level of personal communication and education where people can learn to understand and value cultural differences.*
>
> *Unfortunately, the dominant culture is by nature usually blind to the difficulties of non-dominant groups. It tends to only notice crises. However, when people become emotional it is very hard to create enough trust to work on the issues at a personal level.*
>
> *If polarization has occurred, try to create a safe forum where people can air their differences without fear of reprisal. If face-saving is important, it may be useful to talk more abstractly about how people should behave in an ideal organization rather than criticizing what specific persons have said or done.*

Check the box below that describes the degree to which primitive behavior and polarization under pressure might be a problem between you and others with whom you live or work. Then, using what you know so far and the tips given here, jot down the strategy you would use to deal with it.

PRIMITIVE BEHAVIOR AND POLARIZATION UNDER PRESSURE

☐ is not an issue   ☐ may be an issue   ☐ certainly is an issue

My strategy for dealing with it is _____

CULTURE AND POLITICS

Whenever we take sides on an issue and align our energies with one group against the position of another, we are involved in politics. Most organizations are a strong mixture of culture and politics.

Politics is the conversation which conflicting interests groups have with each other within the larger group or organization. Political interests are often divided along cultural lines, black or white, women or men, young or old, workers or management, sales or production, and so forth.

When a culture finds itself discriminated against or feels its integrity or interests threatened, it will declare political objectives and fight for them. If it can find other groups with similar interests, even though of a different culture, the group may be able to create a *coalition* to increase its political leverage to get what it needs.

The healthy organization has both a culture of its own and politics. Its culture, the unifying elements of belonging to the larger organization, helps it to focus, communicate and achieve its goals. People are pulled together by commitment to the values and goals or benefits which belonging to the group provides. These are reinforced by the rituals and rules, common language, and traditions which develop.

Political forces in the organization bring vitality, respond to and speak for change, and may be used to protect the diversity of human resources while guaranteeing the fair distribution of benefits within the organization.

DRAW YOUR ORGANIZATION

In the space provided below, draw a diagram of your group or organization. Include in it both the cultural factors that make it one and the political issues that divide it.

Where are you in this diagram? Put your initials wherever you see yourself contributing to the cultural values of the organization as well as where you are clearly for or against an issue or political position. If you aren't involved, mark an X on the places where you could make a contribution.

Successful management of an organization requires skill at balancing the cultural forces and political forces which, if poorly managed, could tear it apart. Real leaders are able to bring out the diversity in people and put it to work for everybody's benefit!

CHECK YOUR PROGRESS

Review your goals and objectives on page iv and the update you made at the end of the last section on page 24.

What progress have I made on my goals so far? _____

_____

_____

What new goals or objectives might I set for myself as a result of working through this section? _____

_____

_____

What things did I read about or do in this section that I can put into everyday practice to help me reach my goals? _____

_____

_____

SECTION THREE
MANAGE THE UNSPOKEN

We don't say everything with words. We also use time and space, gestures, touches, looks, and tone of voice to send messages that are sometimes stronger than words. This section will help you identify and deal with some of the major differences in the unspoken language of people from different cultures.

GESTURES

Often we use gestures to communicate with others. Movements of hands, arms, and head help us say what we mean. Gestures are usually readily understood within one's culture, but may easily be misinterpreted by outsiders. No gestures are universal.

Even how one shakes one's head to indicate "yes" or "no", or waves a hand or arm to tell someone else to come closer, may differ significantly from culture to culture. An American exchange student remembers asking a young Bulgarian woman for a date and feeling rebuffed when she repeatedly shook her head from side to side. Her way of saying "yes" felt to him like "no," or "I'm not so sure!"

Desmond Morris in *Manwatching* points out how one familiar gesture, the circle made with thumb and forefinger may have totally different meanings in different cultures and contexts.

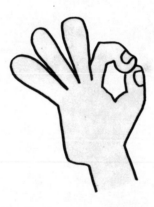

Possible meanings:

A-OK, everything's fine, perfect. (USA, UK, much of Europe)

He's a zero, don't pay any attention to him, don't take him seriously. (France)

An obscene characterization of a third person, or an obscene accusation. (Certain Mediterranean countries)

Please give me change (coins). (Japan)

GESTURES (Continued)

Other movements we make less consciously tell others we are comfortable or uncomfortable with them. These gestures may make us seem rude or threatening, appealing or even seductive—even when we don't want to be.

Something as simple as how we sit or cross our legs may send an unintended message. For example, Europeans are sometimes unconsciously offended by the open way in which American men cross their legs. For them it expresses a crude machismo. Americans in turn, suspect that European men are effeminate because of how they manage this movement.

Can you remember a time when you were confused by someone else's gesture or body movement, or someone else was confused by something you did or the way in which you moved? Describe what happened in the space below:

_____

_____

_____

_____

The following *tips* will help you become more alert to cultural misunderstandings in non-verbal communication.

- *Pay attention* to how others make their gestures and movements. If they are culturally different from you, expect that their gestures may mean something slightly or even radically different from what you interpret.

- *Ask questions* about gestures that seem puzzling to you. If a certain gesture is embarrassing, people may be reluctant to tell you, so ask someone you trust to tell you the truth. When people belong to more than one culture or subculture this may be difficult. For example, men of one ethnic background may not be able to explain certain gestures which women of the same background make and vice versa, so you may have to ask more than one individual.

- *Don't imitate what you don't fully understand.* To do so may invite disaster.

- *Apologize if you misinterpret* another's gesture. Then ask for correct information.

- *Advise others* who use inappropriate gestures which could embarrass them or someone else. Tell them in a way that does not make them "lose face."

MARKING TIME

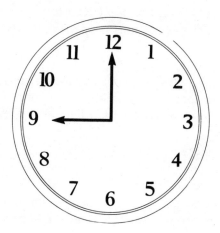

When is the right time? People of different cultural backgrounds may give different answers to this question:

- at nine o'clock
- at twenty-one hundred hours
- at sunset
- when everything is ready
- when everyone is here
- when I'm good and ready

Some cultures count time by the pulsing of a digital watch. They see time like money or some other commodity that can be used, saved, spent, or squandered. Others see only the rhythm, or cycles of growth of people or things.

We're not just talking about the disparity between industrialized and non-industrialized societies here. Just walk from the research wing to the advertising offices of any large corporation and you can see a difference in the way people notice time. Here is a story which a childless woman told about how she learned to be sensitive to someone else's experience of time.

> *When I was a supervisor, I had to discipline a woman who was a single parent for being late every day. She labelled me as a pushy boss who was not going to support her. She was angry at the world and very uncooperative and it was all my fault, because I did not understand the needs of a single parent.*
>
> *We got down to her needs. Her son needed to be at school on time and was always late, and if he was on time, she would be too. So we brainstormed ways that she could get him ready on time.*

HOW DO YOU MEASURE TIME?

Here is a list of questions about time that you may have asked yourself. Check those that sound familiar.

☐ How many meetings will it take to close the deal?

☐ What's her hurry?

☐ Why don't "those people" ever come to work on time?

☐ How long must I be kept waiting?

☐ How can I get his full attention? He seems always to be answering the phone or greeting visitors when I am meeting with him?

☐ Why doesn't she respond to deadlines?

☐ How long do I have to be in this organization before I get to say something?

☐ Why not take the time to get everybody's opinion?

☐ If "time is money," how come I have so much time and so little money?

☐ When they say 9:00 AM do they mean "our" time or "their" time?

☐ How can somebody be so upset over a few minutes difference?

☐ How can he expect me to remember something so far in advance?

☐ It's past and done. When will she stop bringing it up?

☐ What's he doing calling me at this hour?

☐ Why is she sacrificing short-term profit for long-term considerations?

When you find yourself asking these questions again and again, it's a good sign that different cultural values about time are at work between you and someone else.

WHAT IS MY SENSE OF TIME?

Ask yourself these questions: Who am I most like in my sense of time? Do I work in short brilliant spurts or move slowly but steadily? What does the culture of my organization say about time?

Mark yourself and your organization on the scale illustrated below:

MYSELF

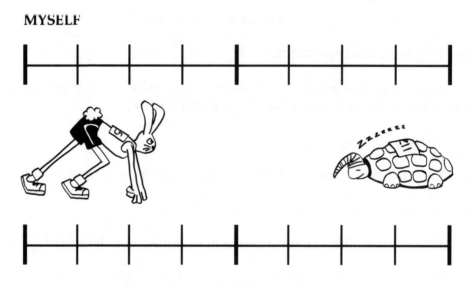

MY ORGANIZATION

How do you handle these differences? Here are some tips:

> *Tip:* *Make allowance for the fact that differences about time can be legitimate cultural differences. Don't jump to the conclusion that others are irresponsible or compulsive or start blaming them. On the other hand, don't assume that you are stupid or insensitive because you don't manage time the way they do.*
>
> *Tip:* *If you cannot adapt to the other person's sense of time, negotiate something that will work for both of you. Many organizations, for example, have adopted a system of flexible working hours, or provided child care and other conveniences to get the best out of their workforce.*
>
> *Tip:* *Remember that culture runs deep. It's one thing to make an agreement, and another to create a habit. Changes here will take patience and persistence with yourself and with others.*

MAKING SPACE

In his book, *The Hidden Dimension,* Edward T. Hall points out that people have several kinds of space "around them." Here is briefly what he has to say about each kind of space:

1. **Intimate Space**—This is our most private area. It lies within inches or centimeters of our body. We normally reserve this space for activity of the most intimate kind.

2. **Personal Space**—This is usually a range of a meter or yard or two. It is space into which we allow intimates and close friends and in which we discuss personal matters.

3. **Social Space**—This is the distance in which we are usually comfortable conversing and working with acquaintances or colleagues while transacting impersonal business. It is roughly one to three meters or yards.

4. **Public Space**—This is the range beyond social space. It extends out as far as it might be possible for us to recognize and interact with others in some way.

It looks like this:

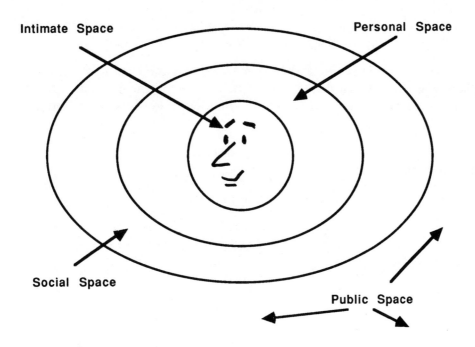

MAKING SPACE (Continued)

If you want to get a feel for what distances are ''right'' for you, pay attention to how close you get to others in various situations. Make notes on the diagram on page 51 about what the distances are like for you.

How large each kind of space is will depend on your background and culture. Getting too close may make another think you are intrusive, aggressive or pushy. Staying too far away may give them the impression that you are cold, impersonal, afraid, or disinterested. Sometimes circumstances change the rules and allow us to get closer, for example, when it's hard to hear, (i.e., when machinery is running or at a loud party).

WHAT IS THE SOLUTION

Learn to be flexible. Know that another may feel differently about space than you do. When you meet people or enter into a conversation with them, stay put and let the other person adjust to where they feel comfortable with you. Pay attention to what you say to yourself about them if the distance they select seems ''wrong'' to you.

If you want to become more informal or intimate, close the space between you very slowly, paying attention to the other person's reactions for what might be ''too close'' for them.

SPACE AT WORK CHECKLIST

When apportioning, assigning, or using work space with people different from yourself, the following checklist can help you manage the situation:

☐ Be aware of what space may already mean to you and to others in the place where you work. What does being in the middle, on the edge, having open or closed doors say to you and to them? What does it imply about authority, about how decisions are made, or about who talks to whom?

☐ Give new people work space and time to settle in. Ask for work space and time to settle in if you are the newcomer.

☐ Talk to others about what feels good to them and listen carefully. Share what feels good to you.

☐ Wherever necessary, set boundaries of space and privacy to which you and your co-workers agree.

☐ On a new job have someone show you around the facility. Don't just ask where the toilet and cafeteria are. Inquire about which people use various space, how and when these spaces are used, and what the rules and customs are. If you're introducing someone new, make sure that you give that person this information.

TOUCHING MOMENTS

> *Shana is about to present her research at a development committee meeting. Peter, her boss, puts his hand on her arm and keeps it there while he praises her work. Shana feels humiliated. Peter's touch felt like he was making her his "little girl" instead of letting her stand on her own two feet. Peter, who is proud of Shana's work, felt he was helping her get off to a good start.*

When people touch others physically it may mean different things. Touch may say:

- **I have power and authority over you**—usually the person with more power is allowed to touch those with less.

- **Hello or goodbye**—handshakes, slaps, embraces, kisses may be intimate in some cultures, casual in others.

- **I want you to understand, accept, or pay attention to me**—pats on arm or shoulder, holding hands will vary depending on a person's culture.

- **I like you or want to become more intimate with you**—affectionate, seductive or sexual touches are often disguised and used in improper settings.

- **I want to encourage or congratulate you**—usually among peers. Hugs, embraces are sometimes mixed with power and authority or sexual intention, often unconsciously.

- **I am angry with you**—using touch to express aggression is almost always inappropriate and dangerous.

- **I want something from you**—touching another to beg a favor is more acceptable in some cultures than others.

TOUCHING MOMENTS (Continued)

Think of persons you mix with who are of a different gender, race, or cultural background as you answer the following questions:

Whom do I touch? _____

What does it mean to me? _____

_____

What might it mean to them? _____

_____

Whom do I avoid touching? _____

_____

What does it mean to me? _____

_____

What might it mean to them? _____

_____

Who touches me? _____

_____

Is this alright with me? _____

_____

Have I made known to the other person that certain touches are uncomfortable or not acceptable? If not, how could I say this?

_____

_____

_____

> ***Tip:*** *Watch what other people do, especially when they are with people of their own culture. Usually people do unto others what they will accept from others—except where power and authority are concerned.*

OTHER KINDS OF TOUCHING

We can "touch" without using our hands or our bodies. We are "touchy" about how we share our private feelings and how we make eye contact with each other. Cultures differ about what they consider *public information* or things that are O.K. to ask others about, and *private information* which is only shared with family or intimates—or no one.

Following are four examples of how cultural differences can create misunderstanding when people share feelings. Think about how you would handle each situation if you were the characters in each story.

Some cultures practice less <u>expressiveness</u> than others.

Bill and his wife Lorraine have a recurring argument. She contends, "You never tell me anything," and "You never share your feelings with me." Bill on the other hand insists, "I tell you everything that I think is important and worth telling," while he thinks to himself, "Why does she seem so insecure?"

How would you manage your spoken words and unspoken thoughts if you were Bill?

_____

_____

_____

How about if you were Lorraine? _____

_____

_____

Annette, a Native American, appears very shy when other people ask her personal questions or even when they compliment her. She avoids answering them, sometimes by silence. The women with whom she works sees her behavior as standoffish. Annette would like to have more friends and can't understand why people aren't more friendly with her.

What would you do if you were Annette?

_____

_____

_____

If you were a woman working with Annette? _____

_____

_____

OTHER KINDS OF TOUCHING (Continued)

Public displays of **anger** are absolutely forbidden in some cultures, whereas in others, people are free to raise their voices and use large gestures.

> *Marva works in the export department of a large multinational corporation, was brought up in an ''old world'' family, where, as she describes it, ''arguing was our weekend entertainment.'' Her associates were raised in families where arguing was frowned upon. They back off from Marva's confrontational style and describe her to others as forward and ''pushy.''*

What would you do as Marva? _____

_____

As one of Marva's associcates? _____

_____

"Eyes are windows of the soul." Our eyes reveal the feelings, attitudes, and relationships of people to each other, but, **"eye language"** may differ from one culture to another. The following example is summarized from "Black Boss, White Boss," from ODT Inc. Look at the confusion that different eye signals give:

> *Charles, a white male, is speaking to his employer John, who is black. John rarely looks at Charles and Charles is wondering if John is actually listening to him. When it's John's turn to speak, he looks steadily at Charles and Charles looks back at him. Both begin to feel like the other is being rude or even aggressive. They close the meeting uneasily and walk away with a feeling of dislike for each other.*

Many blacks when talking tend to look almost steadily at the listener but when listening tend to make only occasional eye contact. Western European and American whites, as listeners, tend to look steadily at the speaker, but when speaking themselves make eye contact less frequently. In this case,

If I were Charles I might: _____

_____

As John I might: _____

_____

_____

MATCH NON-VERBALS

Did you ever notice how you sometimes unconsciously mirror another person's non-verbal behavior? They fold their arms; you fold yours. They cross their legs; you cross yours and so forth. Imitation is the normal way we learn to behave in our own culture. You can see it when children play "grown-up." Even as adults we automatically tend to imitate another to become comfortable with them or to feel at home in a new culture.

Learning by imitation is a slow process. However, we may also consciously work to intensify our rapport with another by matching or mirroring their:

- **Tone of voice**—high or low-pitch, musicality.

- **Body posture**—position of arms, legs, body forward, etc.

- **Breathing rate**—fast or slow, tense or relaxed.

- **Comfortable distance**—once the other person feels comfortable, remain within the range they set.

- **Timing & pacing of speech patterns**—fast, slow, length of pauses between words, sentences, time before beginning to speak after the other has spoken, etc.

EXERCISE
Meet someone from another culture at lunch or in some informal setting. At various points in the conversation match the non-verbal actions of this person. Be careful not to exaggerate or call attention to your attempts to match their behavior. Also, even though you are matching tone of voice and pacing, do not try to imitate another person's accent.

Observe both how you feel and how the other person reacts. *Do not try to match everything at once—practice with one thing at a time and do it for short periods of time only.* Note any interesting outcomes below.

TALK SENSE

Our senses shape our thinking. We remember and think about things as we saw, heard, or felt them. Some individuals and cultures stress one kind of thinking more than the others, though all cultures use all of them at one time or another.

Some people are **visual.** They prefer to think with their mind's eye. They prefer words that enable them to picture and see things.

Others talk to themselves in words that their minds can listen to. They like words which help them hear things. We call them **auditory.**

Still others imagine things in terms of movement, feeling and action. The famous scientist Einstein used this **kinesthetic** type of thinking when he formulated his famous theory of relativity.

The following story illustrates how senses shape our thinking:

> *Three friends went sailing together for the first time. That evening George, the boat's captain, took them to dinner and asked each how they liked it. Walt told how he enjoyed the sounds of the waves slapping against the bow and the singing of the wind through the rigging. Marianne remembered how the rocking motion of the boat relaxed her to the point where she took a nap in the warm sun on the deck. Nico described the magnificant color contrast between the white sails and the blue sky.*

What are likely to be the preferred thinking styles (visual, auditory, kinesthetic) of:

Walt? _____

Marianne? _____

Nico? _____

George? _____

Compare your answers with those of the author at the bottom of this page.

Walt—Auditory; Marianne—Kinesthetic; Nico—Visual; George—a little harder to judge. His concern with taste and feeling would probably make him Kinesthetic.

USE VERBAL CUES

The kinds of words people use also gives us clues about how they prefer to think. You can establish better rapport with them by using words whose thinking style matches theirs. This will help them understand you better as well as increase their comfort and trust. To do this, look for ''verbal clues'' as to how they think, for example:

If their ''verbal clue'' is...	Your response could be...
Give me the big **picture**.	Here's how it **looks.** **Imagine**...
That doesn't **sound** right to me.	Well, then, **listen** to this...
The objectives **feel** appropriate.	Let me **touch** on the timetable.

YOU TRY IT:

Imagine someone has asked you these questions, how might you answer?

*What's the **outlook?*** _____

_____

_____

*What do you **hear** about Jill?* _____

_____

_____

*Do you have a **grasp** of what it means?* _____

_____

_____

SECTION FOUR
AFTERWORD

When you finish this book, you will return to face the hard question of how to get along with real people in your everyday world.

Most who read this book will be living and working in an environment in which the cultural values of white males have set the standards for business, industry, and politics. Whether or not you are a member of the dominant culture will determine how you work to create fairness, opportunity and success in your organization for all of its members.

This section will help you identify the problems of dominant cultures and minorities and will give you tips on how to handle them. It will also show you how to continue learning to work with people who are different from you after you have finished this book and provide you with a list of resources.

TWO SIDES OF DIVERSITY

As a member of a dominant culture, or when working in your own culture, the normal illusion is that your reality is everybody's reality. You see your system as "how things are," and expect everyone else to fit, since you "know best." When you are in somebody else's culture, things are different. You are the one who's out of sync. You may feel shy, wrong, guilty, stupid, or ashamed, even though you are doing your best to understand and collaborate with others. Take the following example which is a common occurrence where women are a minority in a dominant male environment.

Jack considers himself a fair, honest, and hard-working manager. He regularly chairs a meeting with three other managers, only one of whom, Marcia, is a woman. Marcia and Jack enjoy each other's company when they work together.

One day, Marcia came to Jack, angry to the point of tears, and complained bitterly. "At this morning's meeting, Jack," she said, "I was the first person to give a solution to our sales problem. You interrupted at the end of my presentation to let Dwight speak. A half-hour later when we finally adopted my approach, you gave Dwight credit for it!" While saying this to Jack, Marcia is saying to herself, "What's wrong with me, that nobody listens?"

Jack is bewildered. He doesn't remember interrupting Marcia. Now, only because she mentioned it, does he recall that she said something about the idea early in the meeting. He wonders what's wrong with Marcia today, "Why is she making such a big deal out of what happened?" He tries to make light of the situation so Marcia will feel better.

This is not surprising. As Organizational Systems Consultant, Walter LeFlore, astutely observes, "that which is perceived as 'different' is treated as if it were 'less than' that which is generally accepted as being the norm." "Different" means "inferior" in most dominant cultures.

CULTURE SHOCK

When immersed in someone else's culture, we go through culture shock. People respond to culture shock in three ways. Most of us do some of each when we find ourselves alone in someone else's culture. Look at the descriptions and examples on the facing page and list in the space provided any ways in which you respond as the characters did. If you are part of the dominant culture, think of a situation when you weren't, even if it was only when you were a tourist in a foreign country for a few days.

CULTURE SHOCK (Continued)

1. They **reject** the dominant culture and stick to themselves. People who do this rarely learn to live and work with others successfully. *They make themselves right and others wrong.*

Peggy is one of few women in an engineering firm. She dislikes the men she works with and sees them as typical of the failure of white male culture. Men, as she sees it, cause wars, economic disasters and domestic violence. In short, they are responsible for all that's wrong with the world. Any failure on her part she views as the result of male dominance.

When I am a minority in a dominant culture, following are ways I reject (or consider rejecting) others as Peggy does:

_____

_____

2. They **"go native,"** trying to be more native than the natives themselves. This is usually done at great expense to one's self-esteem. *They make themselves wrong and others right.*

Jon Marks (he changed his name from Juan Marcos) is trying desperately to succeed in sales. He had his hair lightened and wears "preppy" fashions. He hates going home to his family. They remind him of all that's backward in his native country. It's hard for him to say no, so he always promises more than he can deliver. He doesn't feel good about himself and rarely tells the truth when people ask personal questions.

Ways I "go native" as Jon does, when I try to succeed in someone else's culture.

_____

_____

3. They **adapt.** They value themselves and their culture but also strive to understand the culture they are in and learn the skills they need to become more effective there. *They concentrate on what works and what is fair rather than on who's right or wrong.*

Lamar works hard to hold down his first job out of school. He realizes that some people don't like him because he's black, but he's found others in the firm who will support him and help him to succeed. He takes a course on black history and goes to a black church on Sundays. Right now he is struggling to learn the large number of technical terms used in the new business, as well as the jargon used around the office.

Ways I adapt as Lamar does, respecting myself and doing what works and is fair to others:

_____

_____

CHANGING CULTURE

Culture is alive and changing. It may look as immovable as a mountain range or as permanent as a shoreline, yet we know that the forces of erosion slowly level the mountains and that each wave rearranges the sand on the beach.

Culture is very much like nature, always evolving into something new and different. No one can entirely protect their culture from change. Even when we consciously strive to preserve certain things, we are actually changing them. It takes hard work to keep alive and share with others what is beautiful and distinctive about our culture, particularly if our culture is not the dominant one.

If you are in the dominant culture, you have a blind spot. Since you think of yourself as the norm, at least unconsciously, it's hard for you to see how your culture tends to distort and even destroy other cultures. Often you don't know as much about your own culture as outsiders who observe you. Ask them how they see your culture's influence on theirs. You could be in for an enlightening and possibly upsetting conversation.

Theo works for a large manufacturer of records and tapes in the Netherlands. At an international business meeting, he had lunch with Pak Tirta, a Sumatran businessman. Theo loudly berated the backwardness of the Indonesian government toward the importation of electronic goods. Pak Tirta was amiable but said very little. Inwardly he was embarrassed and offended at what he heard. Pak Tirka thought Theo was a perfect example of why one must be cautious about letting certain Western influences into his country. Theo left the table feeling more satisfied, thinking that this Indonesian who smiled was a good sign that things might be changing.

All of us, whether in the dominant culture or not are facing a wholesale assault on inherited cultural values by the proliferation of electronic media. This is not to accuse the media of evil intentions, even though propaganda campaigns do occur. It is simply to say that media technology is so powerful that it changes how we view things.

So pervasive are the messages of radio, television, video, and audio recordings, that they drown out the voices of tradition, the efforts of parents and teachers to educate their children in other values. The distinction between fact and entertainment becomes blurred.

It is not surprising that curbs are placed on the use of media by individuals, families and governments in many parts of the world. Such curbs range from regulating computer trading on the stock exchange, where machines actually ''make decisions,'' to banning the importation of rock music. The survival of the economy and of culture are at stake.

CHANGING CULTURE (Continued)

What should we do about the larger forces that are affecting our culture? There is no easy answer. Here are some partial answers. Check the ones which reflect your feelings:

☐ I am alert and aware of what is taking place in the media and how it affects my cultural values.

☐ I talk about it with others and raise their awareness.

☐ I patronize and use media which supports values I profess.

☐ I let my feelings and values be known, especially when something offends me or your culture in the media. I support positive and multicultural programming.

☐ I am active in the media. I encourage or become involved in creating better programs.

☐ I find ways of using the media to support important values of my culture and to learn about the cultures of others.

LOSS OF DOMINANCE

Dominant cultures eventually change and lose their dominant status. For example, this is happening today to the white, male-oriented culture of the work force in the United States. It would be fair to say that in the United States, that most trade, industry and business has been dominated by white males both in numbers and values. This is changing. U.S. Department of Labor statistics and other projections show that:

- White males are now less than half the U.S. work force.

- Foreign-owned companies employ abour four percent of the U.S. work force. In the chemical industry about half of U.S. workers are working for foreign-owned companies.

- Women will comprise almost two thirds of all the new entrants into the U.S. work force between now and the year 2000.

- By 2025, only 15 percent of those entering the U.S. work force will be white males, 42 percent will be white females, the balance will be Afro-Americans and immigrants. Nearly a third of the new entrants will be men and women of color.

- Immigrants will represent the largest share of the increase of the U.S. population and work force.

Statistics may not be perfect predictors, but they do indicate trends. Other statistics, just as surprising could be cited for nations around the world. You can see it in the streets of major cities. The population of Toronto, for example, which was made up of 20 percent people of color in 1940 will have 70 percent by the turn of the century.

CHANGING CULTURES (Continued)

Dr. Lucia Edmonds and Jimmy Jones, experts in multicultural development, have observed:

"Corporations and organizations that do not work assertively with multiculturalism will ultimately do poorly in the world marketplace. They will face work-place disharmony, balkanization of the work force, greater labor-management tensions, higher discrimination case costs, loss of domestic and international markets and loss of productivity."

TIME OUT

Congratulate yourself for having the interest and commitment to pick up this book and work through it this far! Personally and professionally you are learning the skills of future success. But, what are the realities of cultural change and multicultural awareness in your workplace or organization? Below is the ladder which most organizations have to climb to successfully deal with cultural diversity. Read the scale below from the bottom up and check the level that you feel is true for your organization. Discuss your rating with others to find out what they think.

With respect to cultural change and multicultural awareness here (✔) is where my organization stands on the ladder to success:

There is an overall plan and concentrated effort.

Disconnected efforts are taking place.

We have decided that changes have to be made.

We have created an open forum for discussion.

There is anger and frustration over it.

People are actively denying that it might be an issue.

There is no awareness that this might be an issue.

What steps do you feel should be taken next?

1. _____

2. _____

Who will you make aware of them?

_____

HOW TO DEAL WITH THE DOMINANT CULTURE

Depending on where we find ourselves, we may sometimes be part of a dominant culture and at other times be in the minority or an outsider. Use the two checklists below to find out how well you do things which enhance multicultural harmony and collaboration. The first is for those who are in the dominant culture; the second for those in a minority culture.

Check the items which are true of you.

> **Hint:** *The more true, the better! However, don't kid yourself about how well you see yourself perform in these areas. Get feedback from others as well as rating yourself.*

1. WHEN I BELONG TO THE DOMINANT CULTURE:

☐ I am aware that I am part of a dominant culture and know how its dynamics work. I listen to people of other cultures when they tell me how my culture affects them.

☐ I have a philosophy of fairness and I let others in my culture know about my commitment.

☐ I realize that people of other cultures have fresh ideas and different perspectives to bring to my life and my organization.

☐ I insure that members of other cultures are heard and respected for their differences.

☐ I coach others on how to succeed in my culture. I tell them the unwritten rules and show them what they need to know to function better.

☐ I insure that my subordinates and colleagues from other cultures are prepared for what they have to do to meet the demands of my culture.

☐ When I train or coach others I do not put them down or undermine the value of their differences.

☐ I give others my personal support and loyalty even if they are rejected or criticized by members of my culture.

☐ I am aware that outsiders to my culture recognize my cultural peculiarities better than I do and I go to them for information about the effect of things that I do and say.

☐ I recognize that when under pressure I tend to revert to narrower beliefs to make myself and my culture right and others wrong.

☐ I apologize when I have done something inappropriate that offends someone of a different background.

☐ When answerable to someone of a different culture, I avoid the tendency to "go over his or her head" to a person of my own culture.

☐ I make others aware of unfair traditions, rules and ways of behaving in my culture or organization that keep them out.

HOW TO DEAL WITH DOMINANT CULTURE (Continued)

☐ I resist the temptation to make another group the scapegoat when something goes wrong.

☐ I give those from other cultures honest yet sensitive feedback about how they perform on the job.

☐ I distribute information, copies, results etc. to whomever should get them regardless of cultural differences.

☐ I go out of my way to recruit, select, train, and promote people from outside the dominant culture.

2. WHEN I DON'T BELONG TO THE DOMINANT CULTURE:

☐ I realize that, because of my background, I have something distinctive to contribute to my organization.

☐ Even when rejected, I take pride in my culture. I take steps to build my self-esteem and the self-esteem of others who, like me, do not belong to the dominant culture.

☐ While I know that I do not have to lose my cultural distinctiveness to fit in, I realize that I may have to learn new information and skills to succeed in the dominant culture.

☐ I look for and cultivate members of the dominant culture who will help me "read between the lines" to understand the unwritten rules about "how the system works."

☐ When I succeed in the dominant culture, I am careful not to make myself an exception or separate myself from others of my background.

☐ I share what I learn about the dominant culture with others like myself.

☐ I recognize that when under pressure, I tend to revert to narrower beliefs to make myself and my culture right and others wrong.

☐ I sympathize and collaborate with other non-dominant groups to achieve common objectives in the dominant culture.

☐ I resist the inclination to cluster *only* with my own kind of people or *only* with people from the dominant culture when I am in mixed company.

☐ I resist blaming the dominant group for everything that goes wrong.

☐ I share with members of the dominant culture the distinctive qualities and accomplishments of my own culture.

☐ I know how to present distinctive points of view in ways that others can hear and understand.

☐ I can respect individuals of other cultures and treat them fairly even though I may be fiercely committed to conflicting political goals.

☐ I know how to refresh myself from the wellsprings of my own culture when I am exhausted by trying to understand and work in the dominant culture.

WHAT SHOULD I DO NEXT?

You can learn about the cultures of other people in many ways. You can read books and see films. A list of resources which will reinforce what you have learned here and help you learn more appears at the end of this section.

Still, what you learn in books or films can only hint at what other people might be experiencing. They can only give you a rough idea of particular ways in which others might be different from you. *You need to get to know them, not just about them.*

You can travel or live abroad or spend time in other people's homes or neighborhoods. This brings you closer to other cultures. Most of us, particularly if we belong to a dominant culture, remain as ''tourists'' in other people's cultures. We have a lot to learn and we should be polite and very slow to judge what we see.

Neither you, nor anybody else can make valid generalizations about another person based only on what you know about their culture. However, knowing what people value, their customs and ideas will give you helpful clues when interacting with someone whose culture is different from yours.

Remember the layer cake on page 5. There are many variables that may make one person different from another of the same culture. Assuming that a person is the way he or she is only because of personality traits or only because of race or religion will cause us to be unfair. *Every person is unique and has many dimensions. We need to pay attention to the whole person.*

> *Daniel and Andy are both from the Philippines. They came together to work in California. Daniel is exhuberant and flowery in the way he speaks. Even though his work is solid, it took a long time for his American colleagues to trust him. They thought he was exaggerating and covering up something. Andy, on the other hand, was quiet and did not speak until spoken to. Even though he was superb at his work, people read him as being unsociable and not a good teamworker. His manager even sent him off to a communications course to get ''fixed'' so that he could be a better communicator, when, in fact, he already was an excellent listener.*

If we take into allowance:

The Individual

+

Personality

+

Cultural Background

+

The Situation

─────────────────

We start to reach ⟶   **The Whole Person**

WHAT SHOULD I DO NEXT?
(Continued)

The best information comes from people themselves. Try using friendly curiosity as long as you are respectful and nonjudgmental.

Here are some curious non-judgmental questions you might use when getting to know others:

What does it mean to you when. . . ?
What do you say to yourself about. . . ?
What's it like for you when. . . ?
What do you imagine when you say. . . ?
How do you picture it?
Tell me what is important to you. . . .
Show me how you would do it.

Remember, understanding your own culture, seeing yourself as coming from one among many cultures, especially if your culture is the dominant one, is critically important to understanding how other people relate to you.

When you encounter something in another's culture that is unacceptable to you, it is important not to reject or blame the person even though you need to deal with the things that frustrate you. By blaming, you risk creating hostility, prejudice, and social injustice.

When studying anothers culture you may get to know things about them that they don't know about themselves—their "blind spots." It also helps you become aware of what is different and distinctive about your background. Not only can you communicate and collaborate better, but you can learn new and interesting ways to do things and look at things. People who are different can bring out the best in us if we allow them.

This book is a basic guide, designed to introduce fresh attitudes and new behaviors into your life. We hope it has helped you improve things you do to manage your mind, manage words, and manage the unspoken factors and enabled you to understand others better and treat them more fairly. Read it again in a few months and rework the exercises. You can refresh your skills and see how much better you have become at managing diversity in your life and in your work.

Talk to others about your experience of reading and "doing" this book. Get them to read it or review it with you. Go out of your way to meet and talk with people different from you. Finally, complete the exercise on "Learning to Value Differences" on the facing page. It is the most important of all.

LEARNING TO VALUE DIFFERENCES

We need powerful beliefs to impel us to accept, respect, and work with others successfully. Some of us have inherited or embraced religious or philosophical beliefs that make this task easier. We learned that we should, ''Love our neighbor as ourselves,'' or that ''All are created equal,'' or to ''Have compassion on all sentient beings,'' or ''Live and let live.'' Such values are often stated in creeds of faith or in the constitutions and anthems of nations. We recite them or sing them on public occasions to remind ourselves of our basic commitments to each other.

Rather than simply paying ''lip service'' to our beliefs or values, we can really bring them to life if we:

- create a clear vision of what we would like to see
- commit ourselves to living it out, and
- freely and openly declare it to others.

What are your best beliefs and values about the human beings with whom you share life and work in this world, in your nation, your work place, your neighborhood? How would you picture a healthy multicultural society?

I believe: _____

_____

_____

_____

I can see: _____

_____

_____

_____

LEARNING TO VALUE DIFFERENCES
(Continued)

As the world changes, we sometimes learn that what we used to believe in no longer works, or our interpretation of it is "too small," for example:

For over 100 years, people pictured the United States of America as a "great melting pot." Immigrants who were "cooked" in the crucible of togetherness, would come out one in culture, language, and tradition. It didn't happen that way. Fresh waves of newcomers still bring unfamiliar words and ways. Natives and earlier arrivals stubbornly and justly insist on the right to be who they are. Today the challenge for citizens of the U.S. is to create a new image for their future together.

When confronted in the 1950's with new waves of immigrants, Canada looked at the experience of the U.S. It felt the wound that separated its English and French speaking citizens. It declared that it would not become a "melting pot," but "a great mosaic." Canada began to imagine itself as a beautiful picture created out of countless differently colored stones. Today the challenge for each Canadian is to live out this vision as he or she encounters fellow citizens of different racial and national origins.

Think about what you wrote on page 71 and what you learned in this book and from your everyday experience. Is your belief or vision in any way "too small" or "out of date?" How could you improve it? Put your answer in simple words in the space below.

_____

_____

_____

Commit yourself to improving your vision of greater cultural diversity. Pick two people with whom you share your vision during the next week. Make a commitment to do this now.

1. _____   2. _____

MEN AND WOMEN:
Partners at Work   110 pages $10.00

George F. Simons & G. Deborah Weissman

"Although gender issues and roles have been discussed publicly for over 25 years and most of us have heard these discussions, we are still deeply divided. Media, books, articles, religious teachings, etc. propagate images and values about the place of men and women which can be diametrically opposed to each other. Without a coherent cultural statement or policy, the responsibility falls on us. We are the ones who must choose how we will behave toward each other. We must select and bring to life the values we will live by."

George Simons

Men and women who work together on a day to day basis need to develop skills and understanding that will aid them in communicating effectively and in developing working agreements and relationships. This book provides you with a set of communication tools for everyday use. These are the ten tasks you are invited to accomplish:

1. Know the issues
2. Learn how people and organizations develop
3. Accept gender differences
4. Speak with respect
5. Learn from each other
6. Create understanding
7. Come to agreements
8. Collaborate
9. Pay attention to each other
10. Use resources effectively

The authors challenge you to a new vision of partnership--you can turn the pain and confusion which women and men experience on the job into personal power, support for each other, and into professional excellence together.

ODT, Inc. • Box 134 • Amherst, MA 01004 • 413-549-1293

Resource Collections for Developing Multicultural Skills

As the global reality of the 90's takes shape, managers on all levels will be working with a culturally diverse workforce and a culturally diverse marketplace. Commitment to the development of human potential, and equal opportunity for their workforce, is now a large part of the vision statements of companies and organizations.

Human resource specialists are being asked to educate themselves, management and every level of the workplace environment in a way that will promote work relations and will respect each person's dignity and cultural heritage.

This compilation of multicultural materials addresses the needs of anyone interested in developing multicultural skills for themselves or their organization. Addressing the central issue of sensitive self-management, this collection of books, articles, and tapes provides the self-development skills and knowledge to handle people from diverse backgrounds in everyday workplace activities - meetings, conversations, planning together, performance appraisal, coaching as well as organizational change efforts.

ODT, Inc. • Box 134 • Amherst, MA 01004 • 413-549-1293

Complete Cultural Diversity Library

The **Complete Cultural Diversity Library** is a comprehensive set of resources for an organization committed to initiating diversity programs. The complete library includes all the materials from the **"No Frills" Diversity Library**, plus four additional books, seven audio tapes, and several more timely articles. Included is a special "USER'S GUIDE" audiotape which provides a guided tour of all the resources including: (1) how to best use them, (2) what their strengths and weaknesses are, (3) how to contact the key diversity consulting organizations and (4) a detailed explanation of each of the four training modules including: "How to Avoid Stereotyping and Other Pitfalls of Perception", "Gender Hostility in the Workforce: An EEO/AA Backlash Role-Play", and "The Internal SELLING of a Cultural Diversity Training Program."

The **Complete Cultural Diversity Library** includes:

Everything from the **"No Frills" Diversity Library** plus:
Four Books — **Male & Female Realities,**
      Black and White Styles in Conflict,
      A People's History of the United States,
      How to Work for a Woman Boss
USER'S GUIDE audiotape
Six additional audiotapes
Ten additional articles and tipsheets
Four modules (two are new and **fully reproducible**)

Complete Cultural Diversity Library
$425.00

PRIME SEARCH
Practices In Managerial Effectiveness

PRIME, the PRactices In Managerial Effectiveness program, is a feedback system based on reliable, real and readily available information. The areas of effectiveness addressed are Performance, Development and Environment. Extensive information is supplied for ten critical management factors, and the results are interpreted by a consultant. Response Analysis Data and a personal audio-tape assist in helping the manager prepare an appropriate strategy which builds on strengths, overcomes weaknesses, and addresses team perceptions. The bottom line is increased management effectiveness and team work.

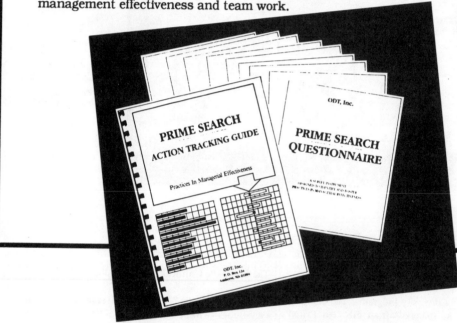

Q: How exactly does the PRIME Search Feedback Module work?

A: You can receive a **PRIME Search** Module from us within 24 hours via Fed Ex (or one week via UPS). Hopefully, you'll take the opportunity to do the self-assessment that comes in the packet (while this is NOT REQUIRED, we strongly recommend it in order to get the greatest value out of the module). Then, you distribute the specially coded questionnaires to as many as 9 direct-reports. After employees fill out the 50-item questionnaire they tear-off the answer sheet and return it to us at ODT in a specially marked reply-envelope. We computer-score it and produce histograms, clustergrams, and a detailed analysis of the composite employee responses. Next, you have the option of getting your feedback "off-line" or "on-line".

Q: What's the difference between "off-line" and "on-line" feedback?

A: Getting feedback "off-line" means that the ODT senior consultant who scored your feedback will personally dictate an audiotape to you (these are usually about 40-minutes long). The consultant will "walk you through" the feedback, highlighting strengths, calling attention to areas that need improvement, and assisting you in interpreting the feedback. The audiotape is also "keyed" to the 100-page *Action Tracking Guide* workbook which you receive with your module. This "coaching & counseling" audiotape will direct you to the self-study activities in the workbook that will provide the greatest payoff for your investment of time and energy.

Getting feedback "on-line" means that the ODT senior consultant who scored your feedback will schedule a one-hour telephone "coaching & counseling" session after you've had a chance to review your feedback on your own. Then, you can have an interactive session, and ask questions, or provide clarification as you go through your feedback. After the telephone coaching session we hope you'll still invest the time in doing some of the detail planning work in your **PRIME** *Action Tracking Guide*.

Q: What exactly is in the module and what do I get for my $275 investment?

A: The **PRIME** Module price includes the 100-page *Action Tracking Guide*, 9 Questionnaires, a self-assessment Questionnaire, complete instructions to implement it, the computer-scored feedback, and either (1) off-line or (2) on-line feedback from an ODT Senior Consultant.

Q: Are there volume discounts available?

A: The $275 price is such a great deal we cannot provide discounts for multiple purchases. However, for large volume classroom training the price drops to as low as $155 for 3-day workshops, and $100 for 1-day workshops. Workshop fees are additional, of course. We also can license you to conduct **PRIME** feedback seminars on an in-house basis. Call (413) 549-1293 for more details.

Q: How long does the feedback cycle take?

A: Approximately 6 weeks from when you decide to initiate the process. Allow your direct-reports approximately 1-2 week to complete their **PRIME** feedback questionnaires, plus a 3-week turnaround to score your profile, interpret it, and get it back to you.

Q: How many questionnaires can I distribute?

A: As a rule-of-thumb, you should distribute **at least** 4 questionnaires. If you have fewer than 4 direct-reports, call us and we may be able to make other suggestions (or you can buy your 2 or 3 direct-reports their own version of the **PRIME Match** Module - see the following page - and save money). If you have more people reporting to you than there are questionnaires in the standard packet (9), we can customize a packet especially for you. The cost is $10 per additional person. Please allow 3 extra weeks to prepare a custom packet for you.

Q: Can I have peers or customers fill out the feedback questionnaires?

A: We don't recommend this. The **PRIME** feedback process has been developed to reflect the nature of YOUR managerial practices as perceived by those people who are the direct recipients of YOUR managerial behavior. In certain select situation we **have** adapted the **PRIME** questionnaires to peers and customers for customized client projects. But this takes some front-end research and is much more expensive than using the standard module. However, some of our competitors do have feedback programs that **are** geared to customers and peers. Call us and we'd be happy to hear about your situation and recommend a suitable source for your needs.

PRIME Match

THE "HOW TO APPRAISE YOUR BOSS" PROCESS

A self-help kit to assist you in objectively assessing your manager's strengths and weaknesses, as well as your own needs, so that you can:

- **create a better working relationship with your manager;**
- **understand better how your manager works (so that you can work better with your manager);**
- **learn how to "manage" your manager more effectively;**
- **learn how to alter your own behavior;**
- **learn some different perceptions about things that could be occurring in your relationship with your manager.**

<u>$80.00</u>

Here's Why This Module Should Intrigue You:

- It's non-normative: It doesn't presume a "right" way for a manager or an employee to be. Manager's are not held up against a yardstick of a "perfect manager."

- It discourages blaming the manager, and encourages employee self-responsibility for managing the upward relationship even if, or especially if, diversity is involved.

- It addresses how diversity may affect expectations.

We think this module could be worth it's weight in gold as a source of "preventive medicine" to forestall harassment and EEO lawsuits. It could be a first round of diagnosis to discover who owns what piece of a diversity "problem", and it can provide a constructive context to facilitate discussion between an employee and his/her manager.

The module is also the cutting edge of our Empowerment resources which were represented in the 1980's by our flagship training program, "How to Manage Your Boss." As the 1990's are the decade of diversity, it is appropriate that this PRIME Match module be the next generation of Upward Influence training.

Some of our clients are even offering the PRIME Match training under the 80's title of "How to Manage Your Boss." Whatever it's called, it represents a way for employees, and managers at all levels, to understand their responsibility, and personal power, in handling their upward relationships in a constructive and pro-active way.

ODT, Inc. • Box 134 • Amherst, MA 01004 • 413-549-1293

People Shape Maps...
Maps Shape People.

What's bigger...Greenland or Africa?? With the traditional Mercator map (circa 1569, and still in use in every schoolroom and boardroom today) Greenland and Africa look the same size. But **in reality** Africa is 14 times larger! Dr. Arno Peters has created a new world map that dramatically improves the accuracy of how we see the Earth.

Maps send unconscious messages about the relative importance of countries and peoples of the world. A distorted world view can reinforce the (false) belief that the land mass areas of the Northern hemisphere are more important. So North Americans and Europeans (the Earth's white minority) have lived with a delusion: that they are the most important people on the planet and they are the central focus in our mental maps of the Earth. Peters is a historian and cartographer committed to helping us see the many peoples and countries of the earth in a fairer and more balanced way.

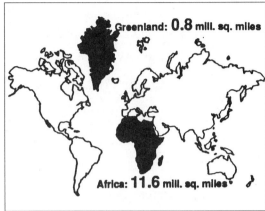

The traditional Mercator map distorts the relative size of the earth's land masses

Peters Projection Map	$15.00
A New View of the World- Handbook to the World Map	4.00
Peters Atlas of the World	50.00

The Peters Projection materials (Map, Handbook, Atlas, and transparencies) are among the most innovative tools for "unfreezing" learners of all ages. Most of us have a fixed mental notion of what the world looks like based on the Mercator projection of the earth we all grew up with. It's a shock to see that our preconceived expectations are so inconsistent with the Peters image.

Peters Projection Presentation Resources

ODT is the exclusive source for overhead transparencies and 35mm slides to be used in conjunction with teaching the Peter's map material. We have a set of 14 transparencies (or slides) available for use in your own in-house training programs. There is a full-color cebachrome slide showing the complete Peter's projection and a color shot of the entire earth. The earth transparency is used to close off presentations. The lines and colors on anyone's maps are all human creations...the planet itself doesn't have arbitrary and artificial boundaries separating lands and peoples from one another. Understanding the interconnectedness of us all is a healthy, wholesome, and healing outcome to presenting this information to any audience.

$250.00

ODT, Inc. • Box 134 • Amherst, MA 01004 • 413-549-1293

ODT'S EMPOWERMENT RESOUCES

Quantity	Title	Price	Amount
	Working Together: How to become more effective in a multicultural organization	$10	
	Men & Women: Partners at work	$10	
	The "No Frills" Diversity Library	$125	
	The Complete Cultural Diversity Library	$425	
	PRIME Search: How to Solicit Feedback Module	$275	
	PRIME Match: How to Appraise Your Boss Module	$80	
	Peters Presentation Resources	$250	

To Order, Complete And Return To:

ODT, Inc., P.O. Box 134
Amherst, MA 01004

TAX ID# 043034359

POSTAGE AND HANDLING CHARGES

FOR ORDERS TOTALING:	PLEASE INCLUDE:
Free to $45.00	$3.50
$45.01 - 75.00	4.50
&75.01 - 100.00	6.00
$100.01 - 150.00	7.50
$150.01 - 250.00	9.00
$250.01 - 400.00	10.50
$400.01 and over	12.00

Order Amount $_____

Postage and Handling $_____

MA Residents Add 5% Tax $_____

Canada and Mexico please add 15% for postage and handling $_____

Other International orders add 40% A.O. Air Mail postage and handling $_____

Name _____

Title _____

Organization _____

Street Address _____
(All packages shipped UPS. Street address required)

City_____ State/Province _____

Zip/Postal Code_____ Country _____

Phone # (Area Code)_____

Fax # (Area Code) _____

Payment by check in U.S. dollars drawn on a U.S. bank, please **Total**

*For orders over $100
call our Toll-Free Order Line
1-800-736-1293
A verifiable purchase order is requested
Fax Order 413-549-3503